Child Custody Evaluator's Workbook

Denise DeNicolo

Brock Haus Press
ISBN: 978-1732427914

Table of Contents

Chapter 1

Contact Information

Court Information

CAUSE NO. ______________________________

DATE OF ORDERS APPOINTING EVALUATOR	
COURT	
COUNTY, STATE	
EVALUATION COMPLETED	
EVALUATION FILED	
PETITIONER'S COST OF EVALUATION	
RESPONDENT'S COST OF EVALUATION	

Children

	CHILD'S NAME	BIRTH DATE	AGE
#1			
#2			
#3			
#4			
#5			
#6			

Petitioner

NAME

DATE OF BIRTH

SOCIAL SECURITY #

ADDRESS

PHONE #

EMAIL

ATTORNEY

ATTORNEY'S PHONE #

COMMENTS

Petitioner's Payments

Retainer $ ____________________ Hourly Rate $ ____________

DATE	PAID	BALANCE

Hourly Rate $ ___________

DATE	DESCRIPTION OF WORK	BILLABLE TIME	TOTAL AMOUNT

Respondent

NAME

DATE OF BIRTH

SOCIAL SECURITY #

ADDRESS

PHONE #

EMAIL

ATTORNEY

ATTORNEY'S PHONE #

COMMENTS

Respondent's Payments

Retainer $ ____________________ Hourly Rate $ ____________

DATE	PAID	BALANCE

Hourly Rate $ ___________

DATE	DESCRIPTION OF WORK	BILLABLE TIME	TOTAL AMOUNT

Evaluation Contacts

Date	Person Contacted and Reason

Date	Person Contacted and Reason

Date	Person Contacted and Reason

Chapter 2

Legal Background

Purpose of Evaluation

Relevant Legal Background

Identification of the Parties

MOTHER

MOTHER'S SIGNIFICANT OTHER

FATHER

FATHER'S SIGNIFICANT OTHER

Child #1

Child #2

Child #3

Child #4

Other Significant Party In This Case

Other Significant Party In This Case

Marital/Relationship History

Chapter 3

Petitioner's Evaluation

Petitioner's Interview

Petitioner's Name: ______________________________

is the ☐ mother ☐ father ☐ other ______________________

Date of Birth ____________ Age ________

Date of Interview: ________________ Start Time: ________ End Time: ________

Current Address: ______________________________

____

Drivers License #____________________

Has your license ever been revoked or suspended? ☐ Yes ☐ No

Explain: ______________________________

Residence Information

Type of Residence: ☐ House ☐ Apartment ☐ Manufactured Home

# of bedrooms _____ # of bathrooms _____ Monthly Payment $__________

Current value of home: $__________ How long at this residence? __________

# of times moved in the last five years ________

Education

School/Location	Dates of Attendance	Degree/Certificate
School/Location	Dates of Attendance	Degree/Certificate
School/Location	Dates of Attendance	Degree/Certificate

Military Service

Branch of Service: ______________________ Highest Pay Grade: ______________

Dates of Active Duty: ______________ Dates of Reserve/Guard: ________________

Military Occupation: ____

Discharge Date: _____________ Pay Grade at Discharge: ____________________

Reason for Discharge: ____________________ Were you ever demoted: ______

Marital/Relationship History

Name of Partner: ____

Date of Marriage/Cohabitation: _______________

Date of Separation: ____________ Date of Divorce: ____________

Biological Children resulting from this relationship:

____

____

____

____

Name of Partner: ____

Date of Marriage/Cohabitation: _______________

Date of Separation: ____________ Date of Divorce: ____________

Biological Children resulting from this relationship:

____

____

____

____

Are you currently in a relationship? __________

With whom? ____

Are you married or contemplating marriage? ___________________________

Employment History

Employer: ________________________________ Job Title: ___________________________

Dates of Employment: ______________________ Reason for Leaving: _________________

Employer: ________________________________ Job Title: ___________________________

Dates of Employment: ______________________ Reason for Leaving: _________________

Monthly Income

	Gross	Net
Employment/Self-Employment	$_________	$_________
Child Support	$_________	
Spouse's Income	$_________	$_________
Other ___________________________	$_________	$_________

Monthly Expenses

Mortgage/Rent	$_________
Utilities	$_________
Car Payments	$_________
Credit Card Balance	$_________
Child Support	$_________
Other ____________________________	$_________

Medical/Behavioral Health History

Are you currently taking prescription medication, have a disability, chronic medical condition, or have you received psychiatric, psychological, or other behavioral health treatment, evaluation, or counseling? ☐ Yes ☐ No

Reason	Treatment	Dates of Treatment

List prescription medication currently taking: ______________________________

Does anyone in this case have a history of/or been treated for substance use?

Please explain: ______________________________

Child's/Children's pediatrician/primary physician: ______________________________

Have any of the children been treated for a current or chronic health condition? ________

Is so, which child, what condition: ______________________________

____

Have any of the children received mental health counseling/treatment? ______________

What reason and treated by whom? ______________________________

____

Criminal History

Have you or any other person involved in this case ever been arrested, convicted of a crime, or are there any criminal charges pending? ☐ Yes ☐ No

If so, explain: ______________________________

Is anyone in this case on probation or parole? ☐ Yes ☐ No

If so, please provide probation/parole officer's contact information:

____

Family Violence

Has there been violence in your relationship? ☐ Yes ☐ No

Describe: ____

____

How often and over what period of time? ____________________

Has there been violence or neglect involving the children? ☐ Yes ☐ No

Describe: ____

____

How often and over what period of time? ____________________

Have you ever been involved in an investigation by a social service agency? ☐ Yes ☐ No

If so, when and where? ____________________

What was the disposition of the case? ____________________

Has there ever been an investigation by Child Protective Service? ☐ Yes ☐ No

Explain: ____

Residents In The Home

List all other children living in either party's home who are not involved in this case:

Name	Lives With	Date of Birth	School/Grade

Do any other individuals stay or live in your home, full time or part time? ☐ Yes ☐ No

If yes, what are their names, ages, and relationship to you?

____

____

____

____

Questions

Describe the involvement with your current spouse, prospective spouse or cohabitant with the children?

____

____

____

____

____

____

____

What are your child(ren)'s needs and strengths?

____

____

____

____

What are your child(ren)'s weaknesses?

____

____

____

____

Describe the involvement with your current spouse, prospective spouse or cohabitant with the children?

____

____

____

____

Describe yourself as a parent, focusing on your strengths.

____

____

____

____

List any concerns you have about the other parent or parties in this case and how that would affect their parenting.

____

____

____

____

Describe your marriage or partnership with the other parent and why it is ending or has previously ended.

____

____

____

____

____

____

____

____

List areas of agreement and disagreement you have with the other party concerning a parenting plan for the children.

____

____

____

____

Briefly describe your childhood, including who raised you and how. Include what resources or support your extended family is to you and the children.

____

____

____

____

What can you appreciate in the other parent?

____

____

____

____

What do you think are the other parent's concerns about you as a parent?

____

____

____

____

What negative things would the other parent say about you?

____

____

____

____

How do you get your child(ren) to do homework?

____

____

____

____

How do you get your child(ren) to do chores?

____

____

____

____

What are your plans for your child(ren)'s education?

____

____

____

____

Who takes your child(ren) to medical appointments?

____

____

____

____

Which parent goes to school conferences?

____

____

____

____

Which parent goes to the child(ren)'s sports events?

____

____

____

____

How do you spend your leisure time?

____

____

____

____

____

What kind of custody and visitation arrangements do you want at the end of this case?

____

____

____

____

____

____

____

____

____

____

Is there anything you would like to tell me that I may not have asked during this interview that you think is important in helping me understand your side of this custody case?

____

____

____

____

____

____

____

____

____

____

____

____

____

____

____

____

____

____

____

____

Petitioner's Home Visit

Date of visit: ______________ Start Time: ________ End Time: ________

Address: ____

Square footage of dwelling: ________________ No. Bedrooms _____ No. Bathrooms ____

Size of lot: _______________

Description of home: ____

Description of neighborhood: ____

Allegations by opposing party regarding uncleanliness, safety hazards, poor nutrition, neglect or abuse, etc.

____

____

____

____

Rate home on each of the following factors:

	Poor	Average	Excellent
Cleanliness			
Privacy of child(ren)'s bedroom			
Presence of books/toys developmentally appropriate			
Presence of other parent's photo in child(ren)'s room			
Safety from hazards inside the home			
Safety of play areas outside the home			

Family pets:

____

____

Observations of neighborhood safety and dangers to child(ren):

____

____

____

____

Overall impression of the home:

____

____

____

____

NOTES

____

____

____

____

____

____

____

____

____

____

____

____

____

____

____

____

____

____

____

Parent-Child Interaction

PETITIONER'S INTERACTION WITH THE CHILD

CHILD'S NAME: ____

Date of Observation: ____________ Start Time: _______ End Time: _______

Rate the parent on the following behavioral observations:

	Poor	Average	Excellent
Parent's ability to communicate clearly with child.			
Parent's ability to show affection for the child.			
Child is comfortable interacting with parent.			
Parent is comfortable interacting with child.			
Parent fosters child's independence.			
Parent sets healthy boundaries with child.			
Parent perceives child's needs.			
Parent's ability to make child feel secure.			
Parent makes child feel understood.			
Parent makes child feel safe.			
Parent avoids punitive controls.			
TOTAL CHECKS	______	______	______

Abilities Checklist

PETITIONER'S ABILITIES CHECKLIST

CHILD'S NAME: ____

CHECK ALL ITEMS TO BE TRUE

Parent's home is clean and safe.
Parent allows the child to love the other parent.
Parent is financially stable.
Parent is emotionally stable.
Parent is able to meet the financial needs of the child.
Parent is able to meet the emotional needs of the child.
Parent is able to meet the physical needs of the child.
Parent attends conferences at the child's school.
Parent attends the child's sporting events.
Parent helps the child with homework.
Parent is actively involved in the child's life.
Parent communicates effectively with the child.
Parent has realistic expectations of the child.
Parent sets healthy boundaries with the child.
Parent is a positive role model.
Parent recognizes child's special needs.
Parent allows the child to express emotions and feelings.
Parent teaches appropriate social skills.
Parent does not interfere with the other parent's visitation.
Parent does not speak negatively about the other parent.
Parent does not express anger about the other parent in the child's presence.
Parent does not abuse alcohol or other substances.
Parent has no serious mental or emotional problems.

	Parent has never been arrested.
	Parent has a stable work history.
	Parent has never been involved with Child Protective Services.
	Parent has never been convicted of a crime.
	Parent communicates effectively with the other parent.
	Parent enforces reasonable rules for the child.
	Parent does not talk to the child about child support payments.
	Parent understands the child's developmental needs.
	Parent promotes attachment to the other parent.
	Parent can place the child's needs above his or her own needs.
	Parent can be flexible about rules.
	Parent shows empathy toward the child.
	Parent is insightful about child's concerns about the divorce/separation.
	Parent is aware of the child's strengths and weaknesses.

NOTES

Parent-Child Interaction

PETITIONER'S INTERACTION WITH THE CHILD

CHILD'S NAME: ______________________________

Date of Observation: ____________ Start Time: ________ End Time: ________

Rate the parent on the following behavioral observations:

	Poor	Average	Excellent
Parent's ability to communicate clearly with child.			
Parent's ability to show affection for the child.			
Child is comfortable interacting with parent.			
Parent is comfortable interacting with child.			
Parent fosters child's independence.			
Parent sets healthy boundaries with child.			
Parent perceives child's needs.			
Parent's ability to make child feel secure.			
Parent makes child feel understood.			
Parent makes child feel safe.			
Parent avoids punitive controls.			
TOTAL CHECKS	______	______	______

Abilities Checklist

PETITIONER'S ABILITIES CHECKLIST

CHILD'S NAME: ______________________________

CHECK ALL ITEMS TO BE TRUE

- Parent's home is clean and safe.
- Parent allows the child to love the other parent.
- Parent is financially stable.
- Parent is emotionally stable.
- Parent is able to meet the financial needs of the child.
- Parent is able to meet the emotional needs of the child.
- Parent is able to meet the physical needs of the child.
- Parent attends conferences at the child's school.
- Parent attends the child's sporting events.
- Parent helps the child with homework.
- Parent is actively involved in the child's life.
- Parent communicates effectively with the child.
- Parent has realistic expectations of the child.
- Parent sets healthy boundaries with the child.
- Parent is a positive role model.
- Parent recognizes child's special needs.
- Parent allows the child to express emotions and feelings.
- Parent teaches appropriate social skills.
- Parent does not interfere with the other parent's visitation.
- Parent does not speak negatively about the other parent.
- Parent does not express anger about the other parent in the child's presence.
- Parent does not abuse alcohol or other substances.
- Parent has no serious mental or emotional problems.

Parent has never been arrested.
Parent has a stable work history.
Parent has never been involved with Child Protective Services.
Parent has never been convicted of a crime.
Parent communicates effectively with the other parent.
Parent enforces reasonable rules for the child.
Parent does not talk to the child about child support payments.
Parent understands the child's developmental needs.
Parent promotes attachment to the other parent.
Parent can place the child's needs above his or her own needs.
Parent can be flexible about rules.
Parent shows empathy toward the child.
Parent is insightful about child's concerns about the divorce/separation.
Parent is aware of the child's strengths and weaknesses.

NOTES

Parent-Child Interaction

PETITIONER'S INTERACTION WITH THE CHILD

CHILD'S NAME: ____________________

Date of Observation: __________ Start Time: ________ End Time: ________

Rate the parent on the following behavioral observations:

	Poor	Average	Excellent
Parent's ability to communicate clearly with child.			
Parent's ability to show affection for the child.			
Child is comfortable interacting with parent.			
Parent is comfortable interacting with child.			
Parent fosters child's independence.			
Parent sets healthy boundaries with child.			
Parent perceives child's needs.			
Parent's ability to make child feel secure.			
Parent makes child feel understood.			
Parent makes child feel safe.			
Parent avoids punitive controls.			
TOTAL CHECKS	______	______	______

Abilities Checklist

PETITIONER'S ABILITIES CHECKLIST

CHILD'S NAME: ____

CHECK ALL ITEMS TO BE TRUE

- Parent's home is clean and safe.
- Parent allows the child to love the other parent.
- Parent is financially stable.
- Parent is emotionally stable.
- Parent is able to meet the financial needs of the child.
- Parent is able to meet the emotional needs of the child.
- Parent is able to meet the physical needs of the child.
- Parent attends conferences at the child's school.
- Parent attends the child's sporting events.
- Parent helps the child with homework.
- Parent is actively involved in the child's life.
- Parent communicates effectively with the child.
- Parent has realistic expectations of the child.
- Parent sets healthy boundaries with the child.
- Parent is a positive role model.
- Parent recognizes child's special needs.
- Parent allows the child to express emotions and feelings.
- Parent teaches appropriate social skills.
- Parent does not interfere with the other parent's visitation.
- Parent does not speak negatively about the other parent.
- Parent does not express anger about the other parent in the child's presence.
- Parent does not abuse alcohol or other substances.
- Parent has no serious mental or emotional problems.

	Parent has never been arrested.
	Parent has a stable work history.
	Parent has never been involved with Child Protective Services.
	Parent has never been convicted of a crime.
	Parent communicates effectively with the other parent.
	Parent enforces reasonable rules for the child.
	Parent does not talk to the child about child support payments.
	Parent understands the child's developmental needs.
	Parent promotes attachment to the other parent.
	Parent can place the child's needs above his or her own needs.
	Parent can be flexible about rules.
	Parent shows empathy toward the child.
	Parent is insightful about child's concerns about the divorce/separation.
	Parent is aware of the child's strengths and weaknesses.

NOTES

Parent-Child Interaction

PETITIONER'S INTERACTION WITH THE CHILD

CHILD'S NAME: ____

Date of Observation: ______________ Start Time: ________ End Time: ________

Rate the parent on the following behavioral observations:

	Poor	Average	Excellent
Parent's ability to communicate clearly with child.			
Parent's ability to show affection for the child.			
Child is comfortable interacting with parent.			
Parent is comfortable interacting with child.			
Parent fosters child's independence.			
Parent sets healthy boundaries with child.			
Parent perceives child's needs.			
Parent's ability to make child feel secure.			
Parent makes child feel understood.			
Parent makes child feel safe.			
Parent avoids punitive controls.			
TOTAL CHECKS	______	______	______

Abilities Checklist

PETITIONER'S ABILITIES CHECKLIST

CHILD'S NAME: ______________________________

CHECK ALL ITEMS TO BE TRUE

- Parent's home is clean and safe.
- Parent allows the child to love the other parent.
- Parent is financially stable.
- Parent is emotionally stable.
- Parent is able to meet the financial needs of the child.
- Parent is able to meet the emotional needs of the child.
- Parent is able to meet the physical needs of the child.
- Parent attends conferences at the child's school.
- Parent attends the child's sporting events.
- Parent helps the child with homework.
- Parent is actively involved in the child's life.
- Parent communicates effectively with the child.
- Parent has realistic expectations of the child.
- Parent sets healthy boundaries with the child.
- Parent is a positive role model.
- Parent recognizes child's special needs.
- Parent allows the child to express emotions and feelings.
- Parent teaches appropriate social skills.
- Parent does not interfere with the other parent's visitation.
- Parent does not speak negatively about the other parent.
- Parent does not express anger about the other parent in the child's presence.
- Parent does not abuse alcohol or other substances.
- Parent has no serious mental or emotional problems.

Parent has never been arrested.
Parent has a stable work history.
Parent has never been involved with Child Protective Services.
Parent has never been convicted of a crime.
Parent communicates effectively with the other parent.
Parent enforces reasonable rules for the child.
Parent does not talk to the child about child support payments.
Parent understands the child's developmental needs.
Parent promotes attachment to the other parent.
Parent can place the child's needs above his or her own needs.
Parent can be flexible about rules.
Parent shows empathy toward the child.
Parent is insightful about child's concerns about the divorce/separation.
Parent is aware of the child's strengths and weaknesses.

NOTES

Suitability for Custody

PETITIONER'S SUITABILITY FOR CUSTODY

How do you think joint custody would work in your case? What are the reasons?

____

____

____

____

____

____

____

What do you think the other parent would say about joint custody?

____

____

____

____

____

____

____

How do you and the other parent handle disagreements about the child(ren)? Give an example:

____

____

____

____

____

____

Tell me how you and the other parent handle a situation when one of you needs to change the days of visitation.

____

____

____

____

Do you think the other parent makes good decisions about child rearing? Do you have any concerns about his or her child rearing abilities?

____

____

____

____

Does the other parent trust that you would make good decisions about child rearing?

____

____

____

____

How do you feel about the other parent right now?

____

____

____

____

How far do you live from the other parent? ______________________________

Do you have any plans to relocate in the near future? If so, what are your plans?

____

____

____

____

Chapter 4

Respondent's Evaluation

Respondent's Interview

Respondent's Name: ____

is the ☐ mother ☐ father ☐ other ____________________

Date of Birth ____________ Age ______

Date of Interview: __________________ Start Time: ________ End Time: _______

Current Address: ____

____

Drivers License #______________________

Has your license ever been revoked or suspended? ☐ Yes ☐ No

Explain: ____

Residence Information

Type of Residence: ☐ House ☐ Apartment ☐ Manufactured Home

# of bedrooms ____ # of bathrooms ____ Monthly Payment $__________

Current value of home: $__________ How long at this residence? __________

# of times moved in the last five years ________

Education

School/Location	Dates of Attendance	Degree/Certificate
School/Location	Dates of Attendance	Degree/Certificate
School/Location	Dates of Attendance	Degree/Certificate

Military Service

Branch of Service: ____________________________ Highest Pay Grade: __________________

Dates of Active Duty: __________________ Dates of Reserve/Guard: ____________________

Military Occupation: ____

Discharge Date: __________________ Pay Grade at Discharge: __________________________

Reason for Discharge: _________________________ Were you ever demoted: _______

Marital/Relationship History

Name of Partner: ____

Date of Marriage/Cohabitation: __________________

Date of Separation: _______________ Date of Divorce: _______________

Biological Children resulting from this relationship:

____

____

____

____

Name of Partner: ____

Date of Marriage/Cohabitation: __________________

Date of Separation: _______________ Date of Divorce: _______________

Biological Children resulting from this relationship:

____

____

____

____

Are you currently in a relationship? __________

With whom? ____

Are you married or contemplating marriage? ___________________________

Employment History

Employer: ________________________________ Job Title: ___________________________

Dates of Employment: ______________________ Reason for Leaving: _________________

Employer: ________________________________ Job Title: ___________________________

Dates of Employment: ______________________ Reason for Leaving: _________________

Monthly Income

	Gross	Net
Employment/Self-Employment	$_________	$_________
Child Support	$_________	
Spouse's Income	$_________	$_________
Other ___________________________	$_________	$_________

Monthly Expenses

Mortgage/Rent	$_________
Utilities	$_________
Car Payments	$_________
Credit Card Balance	$_________
Child Support	$_________
Other ___________________________	$_________

Medical/Behavioral Health History

Are you currently taking prescription medication, have a disability, chronic medical condition, or have you received psychiatric, psychological, or other behavioral health treatment, evaluation, or counseling? ☐ Yes ☐ No

Reason	Treatment	Dates of Treatment

List prescription medication currently taking: ______________________________

Does anyone in this case have a history of/or been treated for substance use?

Please explain: ______________________________

Child's/Children's pediatrician/primary physician: ______________________________

Have any of the children been treated for a current or chronic health condition? ________

Is so, which child, what condition: ______________________________

____

Have any of the children received mental health counseling/treatment? ____________

What reason and treated by whom? ______________________________

____

Criminal History

Have you or any other person involved in this case ever been arrested, convicted of a crime, or are there any criminal charges pending? ☐ Yes ☐ No

If so, explain: ______________________________

Is anyone in this case on probation or parole? ☐ Yes ☐ No

If so, please provide probation/parole officer's contact information:

____

Family Violence

Has there been violence in your relationship? ☐ Yes ☐ No

Describe: ____

____

How often and over what period of time? ______________________

Has there been violence or neglect involving the children? ☐ Yes ☐ No

Describe: ____

____

How often and over what period of time? ______________________

Have you ever been involved in an investigation by a social service agency? ☐ Yes ☐ No

If so, when and where? ______________________________

What was the disposition of the case? ______________________

Has there ever been an investigation by Child Protective Service? ☐ Yes ☐ No

Explain: ____

Residents In The Home

List all other children living in either party's home who are not involved in this case:

Name	Lives With	Date of Birth	School/Grade

Do any other individuals stay or live in your home, full time or part time? ☐ Yes ☐ No

If yes, what are their names, ages, and relationship to you?

Questions

Describe the involvement with your current spouse, prospective spouse or cohabitant with the children?

What are your child(ren)'s needs and strengths?

What are your children's weaknesses?

Describe the involvement with your current spouse, prospective spouse or cohabitant with the children?

Describe yourself as a parent, focusing on your strengths.

List any concerns you have about the other parent or parties in this case and how that would affect their parenting.

Describe your marriage or partnership with the other parent and why it is ending or has previously ended.

List areas of agreement and disagreement you have with the other party concerning a parenting plan for the children.

____

____

____

____

Briefly describe your childhood, including who raised you and how. Include what resources or support your extended family is to you and the children.

____

____

____

____

What can you appreciate in the other parent?

____

____

____

____

What do you think are the other parent's concerns about you as a parent?

____

____

____

____

What negative things would the other parent say about you?

____

____

____

____

How do you get your child(ren) to do homework?

____

____

____

____

How do you get your child(ren) to do chores?

____

____

____

____

What are your plans for your child(ren)'s education?

____

____

____

____

Who takes your child(ren) to medical appointments?

____

____

____

____

Which parent goes to school conferences?

____

____

____

____

Which parent goes to the child(ren)'s sports events?

____

____

____

____

How do you spend your leisure time?

____

____

____

____

____

What kind of custody and visitation arrangements do you want at the end of this case?

Is there anything you would like to tell me that I may not have asked during this interview that you think is important in helping me understand your side of this custody case?

Respondent's Home Visit

Date of visit: ______________ Start Time: ________ End Time: ________

Address: ____

Square footage of dwelling: ________________ No. Bedrooms _____ No. Bathrooms ____

Size of lot: _______________

Description of home: ____

Description of neighborhood: ____

Allegations by opposing party regarding uncleanliness, safety hazards, poor nutrition, neglect or abuse, etc.

____

____

____

____

Rate home on each of the following factors:

	Poor	Average	Excellent
Cleanliness			
Privacy of child(ren)'s bedroom			
Presence of books/toys developmentally appropriate			
Presence of other parent's photo in child(ren)'s room			
Safety from hazards inside the home			
Safety of play areas outside the home			

Family pets:

Observations of neighborhood safety and dangers to child(ren):

Overall impression of the home:

NOTES

Parent-Child Interaction

RESPONDENT'S INTERACTION WITH THE CHILD

CHILD'S NAME: ____

Date of Observation: ______________ Start Time: ________ End Time: ________

Rate the parent on the following behavioral observations:

	Poor	Average	Excellent
Parent's ability to communicate clearly with child.			
Parent's ability to show affection for the child.			
Child is comfortable interacting with parent.			
Parent is comfortable interacting with child.			
Parent fosters child's independence.			
Parent sets healthy boundaries with child.			
Parent perceives child's needs.			
Parent's ability to make child feel secure.			
Parent makes child feel understood.			
Parent makes child feel safe.			
Parent avoids punitive controls.			
TOTAL CHECKS	_______	_______	_______

Abilities Checklist

RESPONDENT'S ABILITIES CHECKLIST

CHILD'S NAME: ____

CHECK ALL ITEMS TO BE TRUE

Parent's home is clean and safe.
Parent allows the child to love the other parent.
Parent is financially stable.
Parent is emotionally stable.
Parent is able to meet the financial needs of the child.
Parent is able to meet the emotional needs of the child.
Parent is able to meet the physical needs of the child.
Parent attends conferences at the child's school.
Parent attends the child's sporting events.
Parent helps the child with homework.
Parent is actively involved in the child's life.
Parent communicates effectively with the child.
Parent has realistic expectations of the child.
Parent sets healthy boundaries with the child.
Parent is a positive role model.
Parent recognizes child's special needs.
Parent allows the child to express emotions and feelings.
Parent teaches appropriate social skills.
Parent does not interfere with the other parent's visitation.
Parent does not speak negatively about the other parent.
Parent does not express anger about the other parent in the child's presence.
Parent does not abuse alcohol or other substances.
Parent has no serious mental or emotional problems.

	Parent has never been arrested.
	Parent has a stable work history.
	Parent has never been involved with Child Protective Services.
	Parent has never been convicted of a crime.
	Parent communicates effectively with the other parent.
	Parent enforces reasonable rules for the child.
	Parent does not talk to the child about child support payments.
	Parent understands the child's developmental needs.
	Parent promotes attachment to the other parent.
	Parent can place the child's needs above his or her own needs.
	Parent can be flexible about rules.
	Parent shows empathy toward the child.
	Parent is insightful about child's concerns about the divorce/separation.
	Parent is aware of the child's strengths and weaknesses.

NOTES

Parent-Child Interaction

RESPONDENT'S INTERACTION WITH THE CHILD

CHILD'S NAME: ____

Date of Observation: ______________ Start Time: ________ End Time: ________

Rate the parent on the following behavioral observations:

	Poor	Average	Excellent
Parent's ability to communicate clearly with child.			
Parent's ability to show affection for the child.			
Child is comfortable interacting with parent.			
Parent is comfortable interacting with child.			
Parent fosters child's independence.			
Parent sets healthy boundaries with child.			
Parent perceives child's needs.			
Parent's ability to make child feel secure.			
Parent makes child feel understood.			
Parent makes child feel safe.			
Parent avoids punitive controls.			
TOTAL CHECKS	______	______	______

Abilities Checklist

RESPONDENT'S ABILITIES CHECKLIST

CHILD'S NAME: ____

CHECK ALL ITEMS TO BE TRUE

- Parent's home is clean and safe.
- Parent allows the child to love the other parent.
- Parent is financially stable.
- Parent is emotionally stable.
- Parent is able to meet the financial needs of the child.
- Parent is able to meet the emotional needs of the child.
- Parent is able to meet the physical needs of the child.
- Parent attends conferences at the child's school.
- Parent attends the child's sporting events.
- Parent helps the child with homework.
- Parent is actively involved in the child's life.
- Parent communicates effectively with the child.
- Parent has realistic expectations of the child.
- Parent sets healthy boundaries with the child.
- Parent is a positive role model.
- Parent recognizes child's special needs.
- Parent allows the child to express emotions and feelings.
- Parent teaches appropriate social skills.
- Parent does not interfere with the other parent's visitation.
- Parent does not speak negatively about the other parent.
- Parent does not express anger about the other parent in the child's presence.
- Parent does not abuse alcohol or other substances.
- Parent has no serious mental or emotional problems.

Parent has never been arrested.

Parent has a stable work history.

Parent has never been involved with Child Protective Services.

Parent has never been convicted of a crime.

Parent communicates effectively with the other parent.

Parent enforces reasonable rules for the child.

Parent does not talk to the child about child support payments.

Parent understands the child's developmental needs.

Parent promotes attachment to the other parent.

Parent can place the child's needs above his or her own needs.

Parent can be flexible about rules.

Parent shows empathy toward the child.

Parent is insightful about child's concerns about the divorce/separation.

Parent is aware of the child's strengths and weaknesses.

NOTES

Parent-Child Interaction

RESPONDENT'S INTERACTION WITH THE CHILD

CHILD'S NAME: ______________________________

Date of Observation: ____________ Start Time: _______ End Time: _______

Rate the parent on the following behavioral observations:

	Poor	Average	Excellent
Parent's ability to communicate clearly with child.			
Parent's ability to show affection for the child.			
Child is comfortable interacting with parent.			
Parent is comfortable interacting with child.			
Parent fosters child's independence.			
Parent sets healthy boundaries with child.			
Parent perceives child's needs.			
Parent's ability to make child feel secure.			
Parent makes child feel understood.			
Parent makes child feel safe.			
Parent avoids punitive controls.			
TOTAL CHECKS	______	______	______

Abilities Checklist

RESPONDENT'S ABILITIES CHECKLIST

CHILD'S NAME: ______________________________

CHECK ALL ITEMS TO BE TRUE

Parent's home is clean and safe.
Parent allows the child to love the other parent.
Parent is financially stable.
Parent is emotionally stable.
Parent is able to meet the financial needs of the child.
Parent is able to meet the emotional needs of the child.
Parent is able to meet the physical needs of the child.
Parent attends conferences at the child's school.
Parent attends the child's sporting events.
Parent helps the child with homework.
Parent is actively involved in the child's life.
Parent communicates effectively with the child.
Parent has realistic expectations of the child.
Parent sets healthy boundaries with the child.
Parent is a positive role model.
Parent recognizes child's special needs.
Parent allows the child to express emotions and feelings.
Parent teaches appropriate social skills.
Parent does not interfere with the other parent's visitation.
Parent does not speak negatively about the other parent.
Parent does not express anger about the other parent in the child's presence.
Parent does not abuse alcohol or other substances.
Parent has no serious mental or emotional problems.

	Parent has never been arrested.
	Parent has a stable work history.
	Parent has never been involved with Child Protective Services.
	Parent has never been convicted of a crime.
	Parent communicates effectively with the other parent.
	Parent enforces reasonable rules for the child.
	Parent does not talk to the child about child support payments.
	Parent understands the child's developmental needs.
	Parent promotes attachment to the other parent.
	Parent can place the child's needs above his or her own needs.
	Parent can be flexible about rules.
	Parent shows empathy toward the child.
	Parent is insightful about child's concerns about the divorce/separation.
	Parent is aware of the child's strengths and weaknesses.

NOTES

Parent-Child Interaction

RESPONDENT'S INTERACTION WITH THE CHILD

CHILD'S NAME: ____

Date of Observation: ____________ Start Time: _______ End Time: _______

Rate the parent on the following behavioral observations:

	Poor	Average	Excellent
Parent's ability to communicate clearly with child.			
Parent's ability to show affection for the child.			
Child is comfortable interacting with parent.			
Parent is comfortable interacting with child.			
Parent fosters child's independence.			
Parent sets healthy boundaries with child.			
Parent perceives child's needs.			
Parent's ability to make child feel secure.			
Parent makes child feel understood.			
Parent makes child feel safe.			
Parent avoids punitive controls.			
TOTAL CHECKS	______	______	______

Abilities Checklist

RESPONDENT'S ABILITIES CHECKLIST

CHILD'S NAME: ____

CHECK ALL ITEMS TO BE TRUE

Parent's home is clean and safe.
Parent allows the child to love the other parent.
Parent is financially stable.
Parent is emotionally stable.
Parent is able to meet the financial needs of the child.
Parent is able to meet the emotional needs of the child.
Parent is able to meet the physical needs of the child.
Parent attends conferences at the child's school.
Parent attends the child's sporting events.
Parent helps the child with homework.
Parent is actively involved in the child's life.
Parent communicates effectively with the child.
Parent has realistic expectations of the child.
Parent sets healthy boundaries with the child.
Parent is a positive role model.
Parent recognizes child's special needs.
Parent allows the child to express emotions and feelings.
Parent teaches appropriate social skills.
Parent does not interfere with the other parent's visitation.
Parent does not speak negatively about the other parent.
Parent does not express anger about the other parent in the child's presence.
Parent does not abuse alcohol or other substances.
Parent has no serious mental or emotional problems.

Parent has never been arrested.

Parent has a stable work history.

Parent has never been involved with Child Protective Services.

Parent has never been convicted of a crime.

Parent communicates effectively with the other parent.

Parent enforces reasonable rules for the child.

Parent does not talk to the child about child support payments.

Parent understands the child's developmental needs.

Parent promotes attachment to the other parent.

Parent can place the child's needs above his or her own needs.

Parent can be flexible about rules.

Parent shows empathy toward the child.

Parent is insightful about child's concerns about the divorce/separation.

Parent is aware of the child's strengths and weaknesses.

NOTES

Suitability for Custody

RESPONDENT'S SUITABILITY FOR CUSTODY

How do you think joint custody would work in your case? What are the reasons?

____

____

____

____

____

____

____

What do you think the other parent would say about joint custody?

____

____

____

____

____

____

____

How do you and the other parent handle disagreements about the child(ren)? Give an example:

____

____

____

____

____

____

Tell me how you and the other parent handle a situation when one of you needs to change the days of visitation.

____

____

____

____

Do you think the other parent makes good decisions about child rearing? Do you have any concerns about his or her child rearing abilities?

____

____

____

____

Does the other parent trust that you would make good decisions about child rearing?

____

____

____

____

How do you feel about the other parent right now?

____

____

____

____

How far do you live from the other parent? ______________________________

Do you have any plans to relocate in the near future? If so, what are your plans?

____

____

____

____

Chapter 5

Interview With The Children

Interview with the Child

CHILD'S NAME: ______________________________

Date of Birth ______________ Age __________

Date of Interview: ________________ Start Time: ________ End Time: ________

QUESTIONS

Tell me your understanding of why we are meeting today.

Tell me what you know about your parents' divorce (or breakup, separation).

Where do you go to school?

How are your grades? Do you have any difficulties in school?

____

____

____

____

Are you involved in any sports activities?

____

____

____

____

Tell me how much time you spend with your mother and what do you do together?

____

____

____

____

Tell me how much time you spend with your father and what do you do together?

____

____

____

____

How do you communicate with your parents when you are at the other parent's home?

____

____

____

____

How do your parents communicate with one another?

____

____

____

____

____

Do you know if your mother or father is dating someone? If so, how do you feel about that person? How does she/he treat you?

____

____

____

____

How do you feel about living in two different homes now that your parents aren't together anymore?

____

____

____

____

How does your mother talk about your father to you?

____

____

____

____

How does your father talk about your mother to you?

____

____

____

____

Before your parents separated, which parent spent more time with you? What did you do together?

____

____

____

____

Which parent spent less time with you? When she/he was not around, where was she/he?

____

____

Who takes care of you when your parents are not available?

____

____

What would you like your parents to do to make your life more pleasant?

____

____

____

____

How does your mother discipline you?

____

____

____

____

How does your father discipline you?

____

____

____

____

Have you ever seen your parents disagree about something? What was the disagreement? How did they solve the problem?

____

____

____

____

Describe your mother's behavior when she is upset about something.

____

____

Describe your father's behavior when he is upset about something.

____

____

Who lives at your mother's home?

____

____

Who lives at your father's home?

____

____

What do you like best about your mother's home?

____

____

What do you like least about your mother's home?

____

____

What do you like best about your father's home?

____

____

What do you like least about your father's home?

____

____

When you are with your mother, what do you do together for fun?

____

____

When you are with your father, what do you do together for fun?

____

____

If you were given the choice, which parent would you want to live with most of the time? Why? ____

____

____

Tell me about your pets. Who feeds them? Where do they stay?

____

____

What do you usually eat for breakfast? Who prepares your breakfast?

____

____

What do you usually eat for lunch? Who prepares your lunch?

____

____

What time do you have dinner? Where does the family eat dinner?

____

____

Who takes you to your medical appointments?

____

____

Who takes care of you when you are sick?

____

____

How do you celebrate your birthday?

____

____

What chores do you have at your mother's home?

____

____

What chores do you have at your father's home?

____

____

Who decides what clothes you wear to school?

____

____

Where do you sleep at your mother's home?

____

____

Where do you sleep at your father's home?

____

____

What are the rules in your mother's home?

____

____

What are the rules in your father's home?

____

____

What is your bedtime at your mother's home?

____

____

What is your bedtime at your father's home?

____

____

Does your mother spank you? If so, does she use an object to spank you?

____

____

Does your father spank you? If so, does he use an object to spank you?

____

____

What do you take with you when you go to your mother's home?

____

____

What do you take with you when you go to your father's home?

____

____

How do you feel when you leave your mother's home to go to your father's home?

____

____

How do you feel when you leave your father's home to go to your mother's home?

____

____

How often is your mother late getting you to your father?

____

____

How often is your father late getting you to your mother?

____

____

What are your worries about your parents' divorce?

____

____

____

Do you have any questions for me, or is there anything else you would like to tell me?

____

____

____

____

____

____

____

Interview with the Child

CHILD'S NAME: ______________________________________

Date of Birth ______________ Age __________

Date of Interview: __________________ Start Time: ________ End Time: _______

QUESTIONS

Tell me your understanding of why we are meeting today.

____

____

____

____

____

____

____

Tell me what you know about your parents' divorce (or breakup, separation).

____

____

____

____

____

____

Where do you go to school?

____

____

How are your grades? Do you have any difficulties in school?

____

____

____

____

Are you involved in any sports activities?

____

____

____

____

Tell me how much time you spend with your mother and what do you do together?

____

____

____

____

Tell me how much time you spend with your father and what do you do together?

____

____

____

____

How do you communicate with your parents when you are at the other parent's home?

____

____

____

____

How do your parents communicate with one another?

____

____

____

____

____

Do you know if your mother or father is dating someone? If so, how do you feel about that person? How does she/he treat you?

How do you feel about living in two different homes now that your parents aren't together anymore?

How does your mother talk about your father to you?

How does your father talk about your mother to you?

Before your parents separated, which parent spent more time with you? What did you do together?

Which parent spent less time with you? When she/he was not around, where was she/he?

Who takes care of you when your parents are not available?

____

____

What would you like your parents to do to make your life more pleasant?

____

____

____

____

How does your mother discipline you?

____

____

____

____

How does your father discipline you?

____

____

____

____

Have you ever seen your parents disagree about something? What was the disagreement? How did they solve the problem?

____

____

____

____

Describe your mother's behavior when she is upset about something.

____

____

Describe your father's behavior when he is upset about something.

____

____

Who lives at your mother's home?

____

____

Who lives at your father's home?

____

____

What do you like best about your mother's home?

____

____

What do you like least about your mother's home?

____

____

What do you like best about your father's home?

____

____

What do you like least about your father's home?

____

____

When you are with your mother, what do you do together for fun?

____

____

When you are with your father, what do you do together for fun?

____

____

If you were given the choice, which parent would you want to live with most of the time?
Why? ____

____

____

Tell me about your pets. Who feeds them? Where do they stay?

____

____

What do you usually eat for breakfast? Who prepares your breakfast?

____

____

What do you usually eat for lunch? Who prepares your lunch?

____

____

What time do you have dinner? Where does the family eat dinner?

____

____

Who takes you to your medical appointments?

____

____

Who takes care of you when you are sick?

____

____

How do you celebrate your birthday?

____

____

What chores do you have at your mother's home?

____

____

What chores do you have at your father's home?

____

____

Who decides what clothes you wear to school?

Where do you sleep at your mother's home?

Where do you sleep at your father's home?

What are the rules in your mother's home?

What are the rules in your father's home?

What is your bedtime at your mother's home?

What is your bedtime at your father's home?

Does your mother spank you? If so, does she use an object to spank you?

Does your father spank you? If so, does he use an object to spank you?

What do you take with you when you go to your mother's home?

___

___

What do you take with you when you go to your father's home?

___

___

How do you feel when you leave your mother's home to go to your father's home?

___

___

How do you feel when you leave your father's home to go to your mother's home?

___

___

How often is your mother late getting you to your father?

___

___

How often is your father late getting you to your mother?

___

___

What are your worries about your parents' divorce?

___

___

___

Do you have any questions for me, or is there anything else you would like to tell me?

___

___

___

___

___

___

___

Interview with the Child

CHILD'S NAME: ______________________________

Date of Birth ______________ Age __________

Date of Interview: __________________ Start Time: ________ End Time: ________

QUESTIONS

Tell me your understanding of why we are meeting today.

____

____

____

____

____

____

____

Tell me what you know about your parents' divorce (or breakup, separation).

____

____

____

____

____

____

Where do you go to school?

____

____

How are your grades? Do you have any difficulties in school?

____

____

____

____

Are you involved in any sports activities?

____

____

____

____

Tell me how much time you spend with your mother and what do you do together?

____

____

____

____

Tell me how much time you spend with your father and what do you do together?

____

____

____

____

How do you communicate with your parents when you are at the other parent's home?

____

____

____

____

How do your parents communicate with one another?

____

____

____

____

____

Do you know if your mother or father is dating someone? If so, how do you feel about that person? How does she/he treat you?

How do you feel about living in two different homes now that your parents aren't together anymore?

How does your mother talk about your father to you?

How does your father talk about your mother to you?

Before your parents separated, which parent spent more time with you? What did you do together?

Which parent spent less time with you? When she/he was not around, where was she/he?

Who takes care of you when your parents are not available?

___

___

What would you like your parents to do to make your life more pleasant?

___

___

___

___

How does your mother discipline you?

___

___

___

___

How does your father discipline you?

___

___

___

___

Have you ever seen your parents disagree about something? What was the disagreement? How did they solve the problem?

___

___

___

___

Describe your mother's behavior when she is upset about something.

___

___

Describe your father's behavior when he is upset about something.

___

___

Who lives at your mother's home?

____

____

Who lives at your father's home?

____

____

What do you like best about your mother's home?

____

____

What do you like least about your mother's home?

____

____

What do you like best about your father's home?

____

____

What do you like least about your father's home?

____

____

When you are with your mother, what do you do together for fun?

____

____

When you are with your father, what do you do together for fun?

____

____

If you were given the choice, which parent would you want to live with most of the time? Why? ____

____

____

Tell me about your pets. Who feeds them? Where do they stay?

____

____

What do you usually eat for breakfast? Who prepares your breakfast?

____

____

What do you usually eat for lunch? Who prepares your lunch?

____

____

What time do you have dinner? Where does the family eat dinner?

____

____

Who takes you to your medical appointments?

____

____

Who takes care of you when you are sick?

____

____

How do you celebrate your birthday?

____

____

What chores do you have at your mother's home?

____

____

What chores do you have at your father's home?

____

____

Who decides what clothes you wear to school?

____

____

Where do you sleep at your mother's home?

____

____

Where do you sleep at your father's home?

____

____

What are the rules in your mother's home?

____

____

What are the rules in your father's home?

____

____

What is your bedtime at your mother's home?

____

____

What is your bedtime at your father's home?

____

____

Does your mother spank you? If so, does she use an object to spank you?

____

____

Does your father spank you? If so, does he use an object to spank you?

____

____

What do you take with you when you go to your mother's home?

____

____

What do you take with you when you go to your father's home?

____

____

How do you feel when you leave your mother's home to go to your father's home?

____

____

How do you feel when you leave your father's home to go to your mother's home?

____

____

How often is your mother late getting you to your father?

____

____

How often is your father late getting you to your mother?

____

____

What are your worries about your parents' divorce?

____

____

____

Do you have any questions for me, or is there anything else you would like to tell me?

____

____

____

____

____

____

____

Interview with the Child

CHILD'S NAME: ______________________________

Date of Birth ______________ Age __________

Date of Interview: __________________ Start Time: ________ End Time: ________

QUESTIONS

Tell me your understanding of why we are meeting today.

____

____

____

____

____

____

____

Tell me what you know about your parents' divorce (or breakup, separation).

____

____

____

____

____

____

Where do you go to school?

____

____

How are your grades? Do you have any difficulties in school?

____

____

____

____

Are you involved in any sports activities?

____

____

____

____

Tell me how much time you spend with your mother and what do you do together?

____

____

____

____

Tell me how much time you spend with your father and what do you do together?

____

____

____

____

How do you communicate with your parents when you are at the other parent's home?

____

____

____

____

How do your parents communicate with one another?

____

____

____

____

____

Do you know if your mother or father is dating someone? If so, how do you feel about that person? How does she/he treat you?

____

____

____

____

How do you feel about living in two different homes now that your parents aren't together anymore?

____

____

____

____

How does your mother talk about your father to you?

____

____

____

____

How does your father talk about your mother to you?

____

____

____

____

Before your parents separated, which parent spent more time with you? What did you do together?

____

____

____

____

Which parent spent less time with you? When she/he was not around, where was she/he?

____

____

Who takes care of you when your parents are not available?

____

____

What would you like your parents to do to make your life more pleasant?

____

____

____

____

How does your mother discipline you?

____

____

____

____

How does your father discipline you?

____

____

____

____

Have you ever seen your parents disagree about something? What was the disagreement? How did they solve the problem?

____

____

____

____

Describe your mother's behavior when she is upset about something.

____

____

Describe your father's behavior when he is upset about something.

____

____

Who lives at your mother's home?

____

____

Who lives at your father's home?

____

____

What do you like best about your mother's home?

____

____

What do you like least about your mother's home?

____

____

What do you like best about your father's home?

____

____

What do you like least about your father's home?

____

____

When you are with your mother, what do you do together for fun?

____

____

When you are with your father, what do you do together for fun?

____

____

If you were given the choice, which parent would you want to live with most of the time? Why? ____

____

____

Tell me about your pets. Who feeds them? Where do they stay?

____

____

What do you usually eat for breakfast? Who prepares your breakfast?

____

____

What do you usually eat for lunch? Who prepares your lunch?

____

____

What time do you have dinner? Where does the family eat dinner?

____

____

Who takes you to your medical appointments?

____

____

Who takes care of you when you are sick?

____

____

How do you celebrate your birthday?

____

____

What chores do you have at your mother's home?

____

____

What chores do you have at your father's home?

____

____

Who decides what clothes you wear to school?

____

____

Where do you sleep at your mother's home?

____

____

Where do you sleep at your father's home?

____

____

What are the rules in your mother's home?

____

____

What are the rules in your father's home?

____

____

What is your bedtime at your mother's home?

____

____

What is your bedtime at your father's home?

____

____

Does your mother spank you? If so, does she use an object to spank you?

____

____

Does your father spank you? If so, does he use an object to spank you?

____

____

What do you take with you when you go to your mother's home?

What do you take with you when you go to your father's home?

How do you feel when you leave your mother's home to go to your father's home?

How do you feel when you leave your father's home to go to your mother's home?

How often is your mother late getting you to your father?

How often is your father late getting you to your mother?

What are your worries about your parents' divorce?

Do you have any questions for me, or is there anything else you would like to tell me?

Chapter 6

Collateral Contacts

Collateral Interview

COLLATERAL INTERVIEW

Name of person interviewed: ____

Relationship to parties: ____

Address: ____

Phone number: ________________

Date of interview: ____________________ Start Time: ________ End Time: ________

What is your relationship with the parents?

____

____

How long have you known them?

____

____

How often do you have contact with them? When was the last contact?

____

____

____

Do you know the child or children in this case? How often do you see them?

____

____

____

QUESTIONS ABOUT THE MOTHER

Do you know the mother? ☐ Yes ☐ No

If so, how long and what is your relationship to her? ________________________________

____

Have you seen the mother interact with the child or children? Based on your observations, how would you describe their relationship?

____

____

____

____

Based on your observations of this parent and her child(ren), describe her strengths and weaknesses as a parent.

____

____

____

____

____

____

Have you ever had any concerns about this parent related to emotional stability, substance use, anger, or other topics that may impact their ability to parent? If so, describe.

____

____

____

____

____

____

____

____

____

____

____

QUESTIONS ABOUT THE FATHER

Do you know the father? ☐ Yes ☐ No

If so, how long and what is your relationship to him? ______________________________

____

Have you seen the father interact with the child or children? Based on your observations, how would you describe their relationship?

____

____

____

____

Based on your observations of this parent and his child(ren), describe his strengths and weaknesses as a parent.

____

____

____

____

____

____

Have you ever had any concerns about this parent related to emotional stability, substance use, anger, or other topics that may impact their ability to parent? If so, describe.

____

____

____

____

____

____

____

____

____

____

____

Are there any additional observations or information that you believe this evaluator should know?

Collateral Interview

COLLATERAL INTERVIEW

Name of person interviewed: ____

Relationship to parties: ____

Address: ____

Phone number: ____________________

Date of interview: ____________________ Start Time: ________ End Time: ________

What is your relationship with the parents?

____

____

How long have you known them?

____

____

How often do you have contact with them? When was the last contact?

____

____

____

Do you know the child or children in this case? How often do you see them?

____

____

____

QUESTIONS ABOUT THE MOTHER

Do you know the mother? ☐ Yes ☐ No

If so, how long and what is your relationship to her? ______________________________

____

Have you seen the mother interact with the child or children? Based on your observations, how would you describe their relationship?

____

____

____

____

Based on your observations of this parent and her child(ren), describe her strengths and weaknesses as a parent.

____

____

____

____

____

____

Have you ever had any concerns about this parent related to emotional stability, substance use, anger, or other topics that may impact their ability to parent? If so, describe.

____

____

____

____

____

____

____

____

____

____

____

QUESTIONS ABOUT THE FATHER

Do you know the father? ☐ Yes ☐ No

If so, how long and what is your relationship to him? ________________________________

____

Have you seen the father interact with the child or children? Based on your observations, how would you describe their relationship?

____

____

____

____

Based on your observations of this parent and his child(ren), describe his strengths and weaknesses as a parent.

____

____

____

____

____

____

Have you ever had any concerns about this parent related to emotional stability, substance use, anger, or other topics that may impact their ability to parent? If so, describe.

____

____

____

____

____

____

____

____

____

____

____

Are there any additional observations or information that you believe this evaluator should know?

Collateral Interview

COLLATERAL INTERVIEW

Name of person interviewed: ______________________________

Relationship to parties: ______________________________

Address: ______________________________

Phone number: ____________

Date of interview: ____________ Start Time: ________ End Time: ________

What is your relationship with the parents?

____

____

How long have you known them?

____

____

How often do you have contact with them? When was the last contact?

____

____

____

Do you know the child or children in this case? How often do you see them?

____

____

____

QUESTIONS ABOUT THE MOTHER

Do you know the mother? ☐ Yes ☐ No

If so, how long and what is your relationship to her? ________________________________

____

Have you seen the mother interact with the child or children? Based on your observations, how would you describe their relationship?

____

____

____

____

Based on your observations of this parent and her child(ren), describe her strengths and weaknesses as a parent.

____

____

____

____

____

____

Have you ever had any concerns about this parent related to emotional stability, substance use, anger, or other topics that may impact their ability to parent? If so, describe.

____

____

____

____

____

____

____

____

____

____

____

QUESTIONS ABOUT THE FATHER

Do you know the father? ☐ Yes ☐ No

If so, how long and what is your relationship to him? ______________________________

____

Have you seen the father interact with the child or children? Based on your observations, how would you describe their relationship?

____

____

____

____

Based on your observations of this parent and his child(ren), describe his strengths and weaknesses as a parent.

____

____

____

____

____

____

Have you ever had any concerns about this parent related to emotional stability, substance use, anger, or other topics that may impact their ability to parent? If so, describe.

____

____

____

____

____

____

____

____

____

____

____

Are there any additional observations or information that you believe this evaluator should know?

Collateral Interview

COLLATERAL INTERVIEW

Name of person interviewed: ____

Relationship to parties: ____

Address: ____

Phone number: ____________________

Date of interview: ____________________ Start Time: ________ End Time: ________

What is your relationship with the parents?

____

____

How long have you known them?

____

____

How often do you have contact with them? When was the last contact?

____

____

____

Do you know the child or children in this case? How often do you see them?

____

____

____

QUESTIONS ABOUT THE MOTHER

Do you know the mother? ☐ Yes ☐ No

If so, how long and what is your relationship to her? ________________________________

____

Have you seen the mother interact with the child or children? Based on your observations, how would you describe their relationship?

____

____

____

____

Based on your observations of this parent and her child(ren), describe her strengths and weaknesses as a parent.

____

____

____

____

____

____

Have you ever had any concerns about this parent related to emotional stability, substance use, anger, or other topics that may impact their ability to parent? If so, describe.

____

____

____

____

____

____

____

____

____

____

____

QUESTIONS ABOUT THE FATHER

Do you know the father? ☐ Yes ☐ No

If so, how long and what is your relationship to him? ________________________________

____

Have you seen the father interact with the child or children? Based on your observations, how would you describe their relationship?

____

____

____

____

Based on your observations of this parent and his child(ren), describe his strengths and weaknesses as a parent.

____

____

____

____

____

____

Have you ever had any concerns about this parent related to emotional stability, substance use, anger, or other topics that may impact their ability to parent? If so, describe.

____

____

____

____

____

____

____

____

____

____

____

Are there any additional observations or information that you believe this evaluator should know?

Collateral Interview

COLLATERAL INTERVIEW

Name of person interviewed: ____

Relationship to parties: ____

Address: ____

Phone number: ____________________

Date of interview: ____________________ Start Time: ________ End Time: ________

What is your relationship with the parents?

____

____

How long have you known them?

____

____

How often do you have contact with them? When was the last contact?

____

____

____

Do you know the child or children in this case? How often do you see them?

____

____

____

QUESTIONS ABOUT THE MOTHER

Do you know the mother? ☐ Yes ☐ No

If so, how long and what is your relationship to her? ____________________________________

____

Have you seen the mother interact with the child or children? Based on your observations, how would you describe their relationship?

____

____

____

____

Based on your observations of this parent and her child(ren), describe her strengths and weaknesses as a parent.

____

____

____

____

____

____

Have you ever had any concerns about this parent related to emotional stability, substance use, anger, or other topics that may impact their ability to parent? If so, describe.

____

____

____

____

____

____

____

____

____

____

____

QUESTIONS ABOUT THE FATHER

Do you know the father? ☐ Yes ☐ No

If so, how long and what is your relationship to him? ______________________________

____

Have you seen the father interact with the child or children? Based on your observations, how would you describe their relationship?

____

____

____

____

Based on your observations of this parent and his child(ren), describe his strengths and weaknesses as a parent.

____

____

____

____

____

____

Have you ever had any concerns about this parent related to emotional stability, substance use, anger, or other topics that may impact their ability to parent? If so, describe.

____

____

____

____

____

____

____

____

____

____

____

Are there any additional observations or information that you believe this evaluator should know?

Collateral Interview

COLLATERAL INTERVIEW

Name of person interviewed: ____

Relationship to parties: ____

Address: ____

Phone number: ________________

Date of interview: ____________________ Start Time: ________ End Time: ________

What is your relationship with the parents?

____

____

How long have you known them?

____

____

How often do you have contact with them? When was the last contact?

____

____

____

Do you know the child or children in this case? How often do you see them?

____

____

____

QUESTIONS ABOUT THE MOTHER

Do you know the mother? ☐ Yes ☐ No

If so, how long and what is your relationship to her? ______________________________

____

Have you seen the mother interact with the child or children? Based on your observations, how would you describe their relationship?

____

____

____

____

Based on your observations of this parent and her child(ren), describe her strengths and weaknesses as a parent.

____

____

____

____

____

____

Have you ever had any concerns about this parent related to emotional stability, substance use, anger, or other topics that may impact their ability to parent? If so, describe.

____

____

____

____

____

____

____

____

____

____

____

QUESTIONS ABOUT THE FATHER

Do you know the father? ☐ Yes ☐ No

If so, how long and what is your relationship to him? ______________________________

____

Have you seen the father interact with the child or children? Based on your observations, how would you describe their relationship?

____

____

____

____

Based on your observations of this parent and his child(ren), describe his strengths and weaknesses as a parent.

____

____

____

____

____

____

Have you ever had any concerns about this parent related to emotional stability, substance use, anger, or other topics that may impact their ability to parent? If so, describe.

____

____

____

____

____

____

____

____

____

____

____

Are there any additional observations or information that you believe this evaluator should know?

Collateral Interview

COLLATERAL INTERVIEW

Name of person interviewed: ____

Relationship to parties: ____

Address: ____

Phone number: ____________________

Date of interview: ____________________ Start Time: ________ End Time: ________

What is your relationship with the parents?

____

____

How long have you known them?

____

____

How often do you have contact with them? When was the last contact?

____

____

____

Do you know the child or children in this case? How often do you see them?

____

____

____

QUESTIONS ABOUT THE MOTHER

Do you know the mother? ☐ Yes ☐ No

If so, how long and what is your relationship to her? ______________________________

____

Have you seen the mother interact with the child or children? Based on your observations, how would you describe their relationship?

____

____

____

____

Based on your observations of this parent and her child(ren), describe her strengths and weaknesses as a parent.

____

____

____

____

____

____

Have you ever had any concerns about this parent related to emotional stability, substance use, anger, or other topics that may impact their ability to parent? If so, describe.

____

____

____

____

____

____

____

____

____

____

____

QUESTIONS ABOUT THE FATHER

Do you know the father? ☐ Yes ☐ No

If so, how long and what is your relationship to him? ____________________________________

____

Have you seen the father interact with the child or children? Based on your observations, how would you describe their relationship?

____

____

____

____

Based on your observations of this parent and his child(ren), describe his strengths and weaknesses as a parent.

____

____

____

____

____

____

Have you ever had any concerns about this parent related to emotional stability, substance use, anger, or other topics that may impact their ability to parent? If so, describe.

____

____

____

____

____

____

____

____

____

____

____

Are there any additional observations or information that you believe this evaluator should know?

Collateral Interview

COLLATERAL INTERVIEW

Name of person interviewed: ____

Relationship to parties: ____

Address: ____

Phone number: ____________________

Date of interview: ____________________ Start Time: ________ End Time: ________

What is your relationship with the parents?

____

____

How long have you known them?

____

____

How often do you have contact with them? When was the last contact?

____

____

____

Do you know the child or children in this case? How often do you see them?

____

____

____

QUESTIONS ABOUT THE MOTHER

Do you know the mother? ☐ Yes ☐ No

If so, how long and what is your relationship to her? ______________________________

____

Have you seen the mother interact with the child or children? Based on your observations, how would you describe their relationship?

____

____

____

____

Based on your observations of this parent and her child(ren), describe her strengths and weaknesses as a parent.

____

____

____

____

____

____

Have you ever had any concerns about this parent related to emotional stability, substance use, anger, or other topics that may impact their ability to parent? If so, describe.

____

____

____

____

____

____

____

____

____

____

____

QUESTIONS ABOUT THE FATHER

Do you know the father? ☐ Yes ☐ No

If so, how long and what is your relationship to him? ______________________________

____

Have you seen the father interact with the child or children? Based on your observations, how would you describe their relationship?

____

____

____

____

Based on your observations of this parent and his child(ren), describe his strengths and weaknesses as a parent.

____

____

____

____

____

____

Have you ever had any concerns about this parent related to emotional stability, substance use, anger, or other topics that may impact their ability to parent? If so, describe.

____

____

____

____

____

____

____

____

____

____

____

Are there any additional observations or information that you believe this evaluator should know?

Collateral Interview

COLLATERAL INTERVIEW

Name of person interviewed: ______________________________

Relationship to parties: ______________________________

Address: ______________________________

Phone number: ______________

Date of interview: ____________________ Start Time: ________ End Time: ________

What is your relationship with the parents?

____

____

How long have you known them?

____

____

How often do you have contact with them? When was the last contact?

____

____

____

Do you know the child or children in this case? How often do you see them?

____

____

____

QUESTIONS ABOUT THE MOTHER

Do you know the mother? ☐ Yes ☐ No

If so, how long and what is your relationship to her? ______________________________

____

Have you seen the mother interact with the child or children? Based on your observations, how would you describe their relationship?

____

____

____

____

Based on your observations of this parent and her child(ren), describe her strengths and weaknesses as a parent.

____

____

____

____

____

____

Have you ever had any concerns about this parent related to emotional stability, substance use, anger, or other topics that may impact their ability to parent? If so, describe.

____

____

____

____

____

____

____

____

____

____

____

QUESTIONS ABOUT THE FATHER

Do you know the father? ☐ Yes ☐ No

If so, how long and what is your relationship to him? ______________________________

____

Have you seen the father interact with the child or children? Based on your observations, how would you describe their relationship?

____

____

____

____

Based on your observations of this parent and his child(ren), describe his strengths and weaknesses as a parent.

____

____

____

____

____

____

Have you ever had any concerns about this parent related to emotional stability, substance use, anger, or other topics that may impact their ability to parent? If so, describe.

____

____

____

____

____

____

____

____

____

____

____

Are there any additional observations or information that you believe this evaluator should know?

Collateral Interview

COLLATERAL INTERVIEW

Name of person interviewed: ____

Relationship to parties: ____

Address: ____

Phone number: ____________________

Date of interview: ____________________ Start Time: ________ End Time: ________

What is your relationship with the parents?

____

____

How long have you known them?

____

____

How often do you have contact with them? When was the last contact?

____

____

____

Do you know the child or children in this case? How often do you see them?

____

____

____

QUESTIONS ABOUT THE MOTHER

Do you know the mother? ☐ Yes ☐ No

If so, how long and what is your relationship to her? ______________________________

____

Have you seen the mother interact with the child or children? Based on your observations, how would you describe their relationship?

____

____

____

____

Based on your observations of this parent and her child(ren), describe her strengths and weaknesses as a parent.

____

____

____

____

____

____

Have you ever had any concerns about this parent related to emotional stability, substance use, anger, or other topics that may impact their ability to parent? If so, describe.

____

____

____

____

____

____

____

____

____

____

____

QUESTIONS ABOUT THE FATHER

Do you know the father? ☐ Yes ☐ No

If so, how long and what is your relationship to him? ________________________________

____

Have you seen the father interact with the child or children? Based on your observations, how would you describe their relationship?

____

____

____

____

Based on your observations of this parent and his child(ren), describe his strengths and weaknesses as a parent.

____

____

____

____

____

____

Have you ever had any concerns about this parent related to emotional stability, substance use, anger, or other topics that may impact their ability to parent? If so, describe.

____

____

____

____

____

____

____

____

____

____

____

Chapter 7

Background Check Results

Petitioner's Background Check

PETITIONER'S NAME: ____

STATE of __________________ COUNTY of ______________________________
Date Received: ________________

RESULTS

____
____
____

STATE of __________________ COUNTY of ______________________________

Date Received: ________________

RESULTS

____
____
____

STATE of __________________ COUNTY of ______________________________
Date Received: ________________

RESULTS

____
____
____

CHILD PROTECTIVE SERVICES BACKGROUND CHECK RESULTS

Date Received: ________________

RESULTS

____

____

____

____

ADDITIONAL INFORMATION

____

____

____

____

____

____

____

____

____

____

____

____

____

____

____

____

____

____

Respondent's Background Check

RESPONDENT'S NAME: ____

STATE of __________________ COUNTY of _______________________________
Date Received: ________________

RESULTS

____
____
____

STATE of __________________ COUNTY of _______________________________
Date Received: ________________

RESULTS

____
____
____

STATE of __________________ COUNTY of _______________________________
Date Received: ________________

RESULTS

____
____
____

CHILD PROTECTIVE SERVICES BACKGROUND CHECK RESULTS

Date Received: ________________

RESULTS

____

____

____

____

ADDITIONAL INFORMATION

____

____

____

____

____

____

____

____

____

____

____

____

____

____

____

____

____

____

____

____

____

____

____

____

____

Chapter 8

Evaluator's Notes

Evaluator's Notes

Documents Reviewed

Chapter 9

Court Preparation

Court Preparation

State the general substance of your expert impressions and opinions and the basis for them.

Chapter 10

Recommendations To The Court

Recommendations

EVALUATOR'S RECOMMENDATIONS TO THE COURT

BrockHaus
PRESS

Made in United States
Orlando, FL
04 November 2026

90200304R00098